Legal
Confidential

Legal Confidential

STEVE STALLMAN

Contents

The Beginning

I took a swig from a premium beer and shuffled my legs as best I could on the windowsill on which I was dancing. Next to me was the Managing Partner of the top tier firm I was interning with. He was in his late 30s, a golden boy of the early 90s, and he leaned over mid-dance to ask me a question.

"Which of those girls would you want to fuck?"

I looked down from the windowsill where we were dancing to the lawyers below - all of them in the top 1 percent in terms of academic performance. To a person smart, capable and ambitious. And looking quite merry as they danced away the late hours of the Friday night in the law firm boardroom.

"Daniel," I said, looking over. "You asked me that last night."

He looked at me sharply before replying.

"Different girls."

He took a swig of his beer and continued dancing, as we discussed the merits of fucking each of female members of his staff from the vantage of the windowsill.

Like Anthony Bourdain overseeing his head chef screwing a bride minutes before she took her vows, I was hooked. For the next 20 years I would work with these people, living among them, exploiting them, getting exploited by them, watching generations of young stars come and go – broken down, burnt out and used up.

I survived. Not only did I survive but, unlike all of my peers I worked out how to do fuck all work (all things considered), became Partner and earn the better part of a million bucks a year by my late 30s.

And have a few screws along the way.

This is how to beat the system. There aren't many of us who do. Most spend their lives in a pit of misery, working their guts out, hating peers, their clients, their staff and ultimately even themselves. They transform from creative types to angry fake men and women who don't make good friends, parents or people.

That's where you don't want to end up.

Legal studies and internships

Your real life in the law starts when you get an internship or job in a law firm while studying. You should really do this, as what you are learning at school is largely useless and will not get you a job or help you as a lawyer.

Do not be discouraged if you don't get the placement you want. Law is full of nepotism and bastardry, so most internships will go to people who are connected. At my firm, where I was Partner, almost every one of the 20 or 30 internships went to friends or family of clients or Partners.

So don't feel bad if you miss out at first, or if it goes to all the students with the highest GPAs.

In fact, a huge mistake law students make is working too hard to get a high GPA. It just isn't worth it. I spent my 6 years at university drinking and fucking, and I still worked too hard. And you know what, I'll never be 20 again.

Never.

I should have drunk and fucked some more. As a fucking priority.

You think that those who got a PhD in mattress studies regret those screws? If they spent their time hiking, fucking, laughing and travelling the fucking world?

No way. They are happiest, most balanced people around.

It's the ex-nerds who are the miserable fucks.

So, as a student, forget being a nerd if that means sacrificing your life in the library. Yes, I know you are an overachiever. That you got great grades. That your mother thinks the sun shines out of your ass because you are so clever.

I'm not saying don't be clever. I'm saying be *really clever*, and work out what's important for you. YOU. Not your lecturer. Not your mother. Not any bastard. You have been put in a system that pressures you to spend your energy chasing a little number on a bit of paper.

But really, what's more important – you getting a higher number, or you fucking your girlfriend (or boyfriend) for 2 weeks in the Greek islands?

Prioritize pleasure. It's what you should mark yourself on. You will never be so good looking. Sex will never be as good.

This is your time in the sun my friend. It is all downhill physically. You will never get those years back.

So do as little as possible to scrape through. Do you think I know what my fellow Partners' grades were? You think a client gives a fuck about what his or her service provider's grades were?

It doesn't even come into it! It's a complete scam. A waste of time. In fact, I would go so far as to say those with the highest grades are the worst Partners – from a business perspective. And make no mistake, law is a fucking business. It's not an exam with your dickhead (and generally clueless) lecturer professor up the front with a shit-eating grin on his broke face.

It's a business. A business won by those with street smarts. With personality. With those who can shoot the shit. Who are comfortable with their sexuality.

The nerds sit in the corner and get exploited. Don't be a fucking nerd. And if you are a fucking nerd, then use your nerd brain to do cool stuff. Get some fucking clothes. Go to the fucking gym. Do cool stuff like travel, cook exotic food, play the fucking guitar.

Become a fucking nerd in shagging. That's what you want your fucking PhD in: shagging. A super high average in your grades should be a fucking alarm bell my friend. It is the fucking canary of your life dying.

Wake the fucking canary up. Save it while you can. Before you get old and bitter.

Of course, you should use your nerd skills to get the best marks possible by doing fuck all. How? By gaming the system.

By means fair or foul, improve your marks without effort. Get excellent notes off nerd friends. Buy them if you have to. Get someone else to summarize of all the work that you don't want to do. Use the 80/20 principal to work out what 20 percent of the nerd work you can do (or access) to get 80% of the results.

And 80% is more than enough.

Get 'tuition' to help with your assignments. Hire the nerd who topped the subject the year before – or better still, tutored it (and marked the exams), to give you the Cliff's notes edition. To check your assignments. To tell you the fucking answers.

How do you pay for this? Get a fucking job. Preferably at a real law firm. Work experience at a real law firm is worth 10 degrees. Because – and I'm sorry to be the one to tell you this – your law degree is worthless. I have trained up lawyers working under me for over a decade and I tell you what to a man (and woman) they have all been fucking useless in the beginning.

In fact, the more degrees they had, the more useless they were.[1]

Everyone starts out useless. Your degree teaches you nothing. The movies lied.

So get a fucking job – or at least, an internship – in a real law firm. It doesn't have the be the big fucking fancy law firm (which is where I did mine). It can be anywhere. Get

---

[1]   Generally speaking, a lawyer's competence is in inverse proportion to the number of degrees they hang over their desk.

in anyway you can. As I said, it's a fucking lottery. So work your connections, and persist persist persist.

Use a virtual assistant to send your application to every law firm in the country, and then sort through the responses. You will be able to find someone who can do the job competently through an online contracting site like eLance.com – probably for 5 bucks an hour. You prepare the application and let them find the contact details, change the email and send it out. Test them first as many are hopeless.

So get your fucking internship. Then what?

Well, first you'll be in shock. There is nothing you can do about this, in fact it's part of the process. You will be in shock because you are not only useless, you are worse than useless. You can't even write a fucking letter.

So what should you do? Well, present well. Buy a fucking nice suit. Look the part if nothing else. Be affable and confident, but not arrogant. *Try and help everyone as much as possible.* This means you volunteer, every day, for every single shitty task you can find. *Every single shitty task.*

I delivered documents. I went to the Land Titles office. I stood in line at the Stamps Office. Just fucking do it. You aren't too good for this work. In fact, it's the only work you are even vaguely good at.

Always remember your primary purpose at an internship is to learn some real (instead of useless) skills and to make an impression. Be nice to everyone. Absolutely-fucking-everyone. They all gossip, and assholes are quickly found out.

Read your fucking work over and over and over. Get your fellow intern to read it for you – check it for you. Not only are most interns useless but they can't even fucking write English. How the hell does that happen? Full of mistakes that would fail high school English. Don't make silly fucking mistakes. Read it as though your life depended on it.

This is your time to work hard. Not stupid hard (all weekend and the like – nothing's worth that). But work at least the hours the lawyers work. Too often I have seen these little babies from university scurry off at the crack of 5 because they have to catch a train home to mummy for dinner.

That's bullshit. You aren't in your little classroom now. I know you're tired because you've had to be at work all day. But if you want them to give you a job then at least pretend to be like them during your work experience.

Go to the firm drinks. Don't get too pissed. Flirt gently (but don't progress) if you are a woman. Bond with the men in man-fashion if you are the man. Follow the Partner's lead. Flatter them by asking about their career and what advice they have for young lawyers.

Listen to their drunken ramblings about themselves and their bullshit.

Smile and nod. This is how you get remembered. And not fucking up the English in your documents.

Try and learn on the job too. Learn as much as you fucking can. Read files. See how lawyers write, speak and think. Your lecturer cannot teach you any of this. They probably don't even know it.

And yet this is what being a lawyer is.

It is generally through internships that you can get a job as a lawyer when the time comes. Try and get a job a year or two in advance, as I did, and travel the fucking world and have monkey sex on every continent. After all, why are you working? Every lawyer would love to do that, if they could.

But they are trapped. Generally in a house of horrors.

So travel, travel, travel while you are young. Travel, fuck and laugh.

Do that forever if you can. Get out of the law before you start. Get a lifestyle business going – Tim Ferris style.[2]

If you don't have the balls for that you can come back and be a lawyer. Probably just to make your mum proud right? Well she has no fucking idea what you've signed up for, or how soul destroying it can be if you let it.

---

[2] Google "Four hour work week".

Being a Lawyer

Once you've graduated, if you really want to scratch the lawyer itch then you need to get yourself a job. In some cases it will be the last stage of qualification. In other cases you will be a lawyer before you begin, on paper. I say on paper because the truth is you are fucking useless. Don't ever forget that.

You are fucking useless, and you are not a lawyer. Not even close.

You are a pain in the ass, that's what you are. A useless pain in the ass. The only way anyone in their right mind would spend time with you is if they have a sense of training duty (not many do), they have some dog work to give you or are on a junior lawyer power trip. Some may want to fuck you (well, if you are an attractive woman, *everyone* will want to fuck you), but for the moment let's just say that is a bad idea so stay professional and flirt just enough to be given the work.

Be everyone's friend at the start. You finish in this game with zero friends. And truth be told you are never anyone's friend. But your primary goal when you start out is to learn and become part of the gang.

Learn learn learn.

Who do you learn from? Whoever is good at their job. Hand out with that person. Be their bitch. Do everything you fucking can to make their life easier. That is your job. Making their life fucking easier.

Impress them by working hard, at least at the start. You don't know shit. You are worse than useless. They, by comparison, have skills people pay big bucks for. So learn how to be a lawyer from good lawyers.

Don't get into research. Don't bother with external seminars, or internal for that matter. You have had enough of that at law school. What you want it rock solid hands on experience. You want to peek out from behind the skirt of some shit hot lawyer and learn everything that bastard has to teach.

If you do that with say 3 or 4 hotshots, for, say, 3 years, then there is a chance if you haven't spread yourself too thin that you might even be good for something. If you have done a bit of this and a bit of that you will be largely useless still, although in your own mind you're probably a superstar.

Drop the arrogance. Drop the superstar routine.

Bond with your peer group. Drink with them. Discuss things with them. Strategize (although to be honest your ability to play is very limited). Get intel. This is all good training, and if you are in a particularly revolting area you may need the support just to survive.

You shouldn't worry about money at this stage. Money works itself out in time. What you want to do is learn your trade, even if you abandon it.

Speaking of which, you should seriously consider getting out of the law as soon as you can. *As soon as you can.* The law is a horrible business that will ruin your health and corrupt your soul.

If you survive you will be bitter and revolting as a person. And pretty much useless at anything other than your area. You will be detached from life. You will scorn normal, beautiful people. Any creativity you ever had will be crushed and you will truly become a shell of the person you were at 23.

Get out as soon as you can.

Don't fall for the lifestyle trap. Clear any debts you have as a 100% priority. Debt is what ensnares lawyers into a life of misery. Student debt to start with. But then lifestyle debt.

Prioritize your debt. Do NOT increase your lifestyle. Everyone does. It's a trap. It's false hope. If you have any debt at all it's a complete fraud.

You are not a success.

You see that 40 year old plumber – yes, the fit, down to earth guy, with a beautiful wife and lots of friends and the paid off house and car? He's a success. You, with your fancy suit and big words, and lots of debt. You're nothing of the sort. You're a wanker at best. A deluded one.

Clear the debt.

Keep living the way you were living as a student. The goal is to clear the debt and save up some money to give you options. Options including getting the fuck out of the law, starting a lifestyle business or better still taking your girl (or guy) and travelling through South East Asia or South America for 18 months.

Get out, get out, get out.

Most people ignore this advice. If someone had told me this, I would have ignored it too. The path most young lawyers take is to immediately spend what they earn, and then some, on lifestyle: fancy accommodation and booze, mainly.

Their health goes to shit. They put on weight. Smash their liver and brains with booze and other drugs. And within a few years become a version of themselves that would have filled the younger them with disgust.

All the time while the debt mounts.

But back to fucking. Needless to say, you should have as much sex as you can in your life. Think of all the old fucks you know. Especially all your grandma's friends. You think they like sitting in their own filth in a retirement village?

No, they wish they were young and beautiful, and fucking.

Of course they do. That's all anyone thinks, deep down. Well you don't have to search that deeply for men. All men want to fuck, all day. Women want affection, and fucking is an awesome form of this.

So fuck as much as you can. Keep fit. Fuck. Stay out of debt. And learn as much as you can from a real lawyer in the hope you become one.

Of course, you don't want to be seen as a slut. Life's a bitch isn't it? One year at one of my firms the summer clerks had to perform at a local theatre, you know, because they were so creative and all. There was a lowly theatre guy there who helped them get set up and so on. There must have been a few drinks involved because mid performance a curtain to the side of the stage was drawn and one of the beautiful young hopefuls was seen, by the whole audience, in, well, let's just say a compromising position that involved the theater guy looking very pleased with himself.

She ran out of the theatre and never returned to work.

So as much as it pains me to say it, keep the fucking to outside of work hours and work functions.[3]

A final tip for young women lawyers who are getting hit on or who don't know what they are doing: *when in doubt, glare*. Glare to co-workers. Glare in meetings. Glare at other lawyers. It will put people in their place, and they will assume you know everything and are angry with what you are hearing. It is the application of this advice that leads to the perception that senior woman lawyers are cold heartless bitches. But guess what, it works.[4]

---

[3]   If you have any spine whatsoever you will ignore this advice.

[4]   As does speaking slowly. Idiots babble.

Climbing the greasy pole

Within a few years most of your peers will have taken everyone's advice, or listened to their heart, and left the law just as they became vaguely competent. A few, generally those who lack imagination or options, will remain.[5]

Of course, knowing that almost every one of your peers will quit gives you a simple way to outperform them – don't quit. Even at a young age I used to swan off at 6.00 at night when everyone else was beavering away until late into the evening. A few years later I was the only one who remained, with the biggest pay packet, naturally.[6]

Other strategies present themselves once you know what you are doing legally. While I am all for becoming really good at some area of the law, the last, absolutely last thing you want to do is be the workhorse who stays back late at night rotting in a corner. That's what mugs do and law firms are full of them.

---

[5] Hence the expression: survival of the dullest.

[6] No matter what they say pay is determined by reference to years of experience (for at least the first 5 years). So there's not really much point busting your ass. You're better off being at the bottom of pay for your group, rather than the top, if being at the bottom means you can have a life. Let the nerds pay for the bonus with their souls - you're getting more sex.

Don't be famous for your work ethic. That's a game you cannot win. Instead be famous for being good at something, preferably something esoteric and impenetrable to everyone else (remember attaching yourself to someone who knew what they were doing? Hopefully you learnt their tricks.)

Confuse the elders with smoke and mirrors

Being famous should be a priority. First, make sure the Partners know you. Generally they won't. I knew one guy who formed a wine club, and every month pooled the money of the members to buy lots of interesting, premium wine and then split it among the members. Membership was limited to the most powerful members of the firm.

Instant profile and goodwill. Clever.

The next thing to do is to use the media to your advantage. Be relentless. Whenever you see a topical issue, try and comment on it. Try and get in print at least once a month. I don't mean nerd-burger journals. Stay out of them – they are too much work and frankly who reads them? Students and judges? What a waste of time.

Get into mainstream media and crappy legal rags. Write an accessible article about something difficult, taking a confident practical approach with clear direction. Don't compete with the army of nerds at the big firms, on obvious cases for example. Look for the strange case, or, even better, an overseas case that has been commented on by people smarter than you there, but not in your own jurisdiction. Mainstream media particularly love scare stories after a concrete example so if you bring it to a journalist's attention and then give him some quotes you've done his work for him (or her).

If you can't access the firm's PR provider then think about spending your own money to get access to the media if you can't yourself.[7] It doesn't even have to be local. Get every article scanned and email it around to your superiors. If possible, get it listed in the weekly or monthly firm newsletter.

Depending on your position, there is a wonderful opportunity here to be associated with and get the attention of someone powerful. How? By asking if he or she wants to be listed as a co-author. You do all the work and make him look good.

In fact, that's an important rule right there, both for clients (throughout your career) and for Partners (before you are one): make them look good. They will love you for it. People, at least the people you are dealing with, aren't stupid. Most know which way their bread is buttered and they also know who makes them look good.

Make them look good.

If you slam away on the media for years it confuses the elders. You must be important right? They have been slaving away for decades and nobody writes shit about them. This is

---

[7]   The same logic applies to buying drinks and lunch for junior staff while you are on the way up. Who buys this stuff? The boss, that's who. Invest a couple of grand a year in acting like the boss and people will treat you like one, do your work and get you pay rises that far exceed your investment. Smart.

particularly handy if you are not performing in other areas, like billing. A public profile also makes you more difficult to fire. They fear the fallout. It's easier to get rid of the guy with no profile. Nobody gives a shit that he just spent the better part of his 20s and 30s working his guts out. He's gone.

So be the guy with the profile. Eventually, they will believe the bullshit. You might start to as well. Your clients too, when they google you (which they will).

Don't have dogs and bark yourself

Surviving from lawyer to Partner is a marathon not a sprint. You will need to sit there for literally fucking years while your life ticks away, which is a long time to be working your ass off. Too long.

Here's a tip. Don't do the fucking work. As offensive as it sounds, lawyers are divided into finders, minders and grinders. While you want to learn the hands on, you don't want to kill yourself doing it (being a grinder). Fuck that shit. You'll go mad, literally fucking mad, if you try and do that for years.

Become a minder – minding grinders, as soon as possible. As soon as you are able, get people to do shit for you. Every fucking thing. As a young fool I once asked a Partner if he knew how to use a typewriter (yes, it was a long time ago). He just looked at me and smiled and said, "Why have dogs and bark yourself?" I was outraged, but he was dead right. Give all of your work to someone else. Save the juicy bits for yourself sure, if you enjoy it. But otherwise give every fucking thing – even the simplest letter – to someone else.

This is more enjoyable than churning it out yourself, plus, if you have the work, it lets you leverage more managed fees than you could do if you just plugged away at it. Want a million dollar practice? Then get those fuckers working.

You'll actually find you'll become a better lawyer teaching others too. See the big picture, and all that sort of shit.

Do not be afraid of killing the goose that lays the golden egg. Law is an absolutely horrific soul destroying bitch. It is impossible for you just to grunt it out for decades. You need to use others as stepping stones to survive. Tap into their enthusiasm; their youth; their keenness and their desire to please. Work them senseless. Then work them some more.

You should get 3 to 5 years out of a normal high achiever before they crash and burn: permanently fucked up by their experience. More, if they are deranged[8] or can thrash their own minions.

Of course, the last stage of mentorship is absolute: the mentee tells the mentor to go fuck themselves. This is inevitable, no matter how keen they seem at first. This means you need to plan for it, with other workers with less experience in the wings.

When they go, hopefully they will resign. Often the strategy is to place them into a client but the truth is they hate you and will never feed you work (at least, not more

---

[8] Almost every long term survivor in a top firm has serious mental issues. I'm 100% serious about this. In another life many of them would have been sociopaths or whatever is the right term for a soulless dictator who sees himself or herself as king and has no concern for the wellbeing of others whatsoever.

than once). They want to be seen as all grown up, and that can never happen with you as a boss figure.

There is a risk that your enemies within the firm will use a disgruntled employee against you, so it's best to get rid of them as soon as you detect dissent. Up or out never used to make sense to me, but it's something you need to enforce ruthlessly. Get rid of everyone within 5 years of hiring them. It's much safer.

Better they be disappointed than you

People will place unreasonable demands on you both as a junior lawyer and then as the person responsible for service delivery. As a high achieving person, the temptation will be to meet this deadline, even if it means impinging on your personal life and private time, which generally fucks you up and if nothing else is extremely frustrating and upsetting.

So what do you do when faced with a weekend of work to meet some fuckwit's deadline?

One of two things will happen (assuming you can't delegate).

First, you work on the weekend, making you disappointed. You never get the weekend back. This eventually becomes habitual and you have no weekends.

Second, you don't work on the weekend, making someone else disappointed. You keep your weekend, and every weekend after that.

The rule is this: *better they be disappointed than you*. Their crappy deadline? Unless you work for merchant bankers (don't), or it is a court imposed deadline (normally things aren't that tight), then any deadline is merely a commercial expectation that can be managed.

And, as I said, better they be disappointed than you. That's what it comes down to – your precious weekend, or they, what, get it Tuesday instead of Monday? Who cares. And if they do care, they really really care, well, get some new clients. Don't be the service provider who always meets every deadline. Almost none do; why ruin your life?

Of course, don't tell your juniors this. Make them work their fucking weekends. They are only around for a few years, after all.

Talk your competition out over time

Ultimately the money can only be dished out to those who remain. Work at talking out your competitors. Use terms like survival of the dullest. Send articles that highlight entrepreneurial success and the statistics of becoming a partner. Be the little voice in their head that tells them to get out.

Most of them will.

Don't shit in your nest

How tempting it is. You have finally reached a position of authority, which, for reasons only known to women, means that they will fuck you. I've had secretaries fight over me, lawyers lead me astray – really astray - after long lunches, and even had one very fit young lawyer psychopath flash her goods at me for 20 minutes in my office after I got upset with her.[9]

So, what does a man do with all of this?

Well, the golden rule is don't shit in your nest (or, if you prefer, don't shit where you eat).

Of course, who dares wins and I don't regret a fucking thing. But it's risky behavior. I transferred one girl who was, let's say, a little too keen, the week after our indiscretion. It was the end of her career in our area, but it could well have been the end of mine.

Never trust them. Even when you have been intimate with them. *Especially* when you have been intimate with them.

---

[9] Yes, her *goods*. Very tidy. Blew my fucking mind too.

One way to succeed in the law is to not give a fuck, and I guess if you truly don't give a fuck then you will take advantage of every opportunity that comes your way. But be aware this may be problematic over time, and is generally not a great idea if you want to survive.

Better your pocket than theirs

Never forget, the only reason you put yourself through all of this shit – the *only reason* – is for cash. Trust me, it's the only reason all those other fuckwits are there. Any talk of ethics or calling or any such crap is just that – crap. You will never work with a group of more soulless and selfish egomaniacs in all of your life. They are only there for cash and you should be too.

Don't be stupid about it. Take the better job initially. Get in with the person who can teach you first up. But after you've settled, make sure you ask for money and get it. There is more money in a law firm than you can imagine. And it's better off in your pocket than theirs.

So find out what you are worth. Jump firms if you have to in order to keep your salary going up. Be aggressive but polite when it comes to pay negotiations – and it is a negotiation, you pussy. Tell them you're going through a period in your life when money is important to you; that you are looking to substantially increase your income in the next 12 months. Get important then hint you might leave unless they throw a bag of cash to you.

And leave if they don't. Those fucks wouldn't give a shit if you died in your office. Make sure you get paid as much as possible.

I did fuck all and pushed and pushed for cash. My salary went up over 20 fold in 13 years. You should aim for the same.

Peer out from behind someone's skirt and eat the crumbs from their table

Unless you are a swinging big dick, and can jag all of the clients, then you will need to find a powerful person to support you in your ascension. That is, use a combination of smoke and mirrors and jedi mind tricks to get at least one powerful person on side.

Be his or her bitch. Make him or her look good. Always praise them publically (and in those stupid surveys you fill out – make sure they can tell it's you). Take all of their shitty work.

Be an important part of his or her team, and service the shit out of their clients.

Because, even though the souls of these people are black, and they will never find happiness in life, they are logical and egotistical. Chances are they like having their work done for them by a keen and smart person such as yourself. They like having someone in the ranks who supports them, even from below. So it really is a mutual backscratching exercise. And if they don't scratch your back hard enough by way of cash and protection from horror, then fuck them off and find someone who will.

I did that with a lazy incompetent megalomaniac for many years and it served me very well. Of course, they will end up knifing you (unless you turn into one of them, and end up knifing them), but if you can benefit from the ride then it's worth the hand up into the boys club.

Keeping your head below the parapet

You want to raise your profile as part of the smoke and mirrors campaign but once you are on track then it helps to be a small target. This means, paradoxically, keeping a low profile (apart from strategic media or lecturing). Tick all the stupid boxes they have in their systems (file audits, and the like) and don't be outspoken. Just nod your head when the fuckwits go on and on and keep stashing the cash away until your exit.

People who disagree with the powerful have short life spans. Be different enough to get on the cash but be conformant enough to survive and not be an obvious target.

Budget is a tough one. Obviously it is better for long term survival if you make it, and in some firms that is non-negotiable. If mentally you can't even do one more bit of actual work yourself (it happens) or don't even have the work (it happens too) then that is problematic. You need to work the smoke and mirrors angle hard: lots of national and local media (including TV), internal training, even precedent development – particularly if it has its own budget.[10]

Generally not smashing the numbers (or even making your budget) will see you knifed in the end. But then everyone is knifed in the end, and if you've managed to do fuck all along the way then the joke's on them.

Of course, all of your political work should be done in the shadows. Watch the elders in meetings (if you are a Partner): no real debate occurs. It is all a farce played out for the record and for the slow witted. Every single decision is made before people walk into the room. Every one.

So learn from these people. Never debate anything publically. It only makes you look naive. Work via whispers and influence. That powerful person whose skirt you are peeking out from behind? They are a good place to start.

Sometimes the strategy is a longer term one. In fact, it almost always is. If you get promoted, or knifed, it is normally something that has been in the works for years before it happens. Every single thing is in place and there is nothing you can do about it.

If you give people enough rope they will usually hang themselves over time. Often the elders wait for that rather than creating a spectacle and risking conflict early on.

---

[10]   That is, if fake work counts for some fucked up reason as real work, then suck that well until it is dry baby.

Everyone is allowed at least one breakdown

The law will fuck you up. That's why you should try and do something else. If you don't, then you will have at least one breakdown. So don't beat yourself up. It may manifest itself in a number of ways. You may not be able to go to work. You may get to work and find you have to go home suddenly.

If you are a woman you will cry, and probably often.

Try not to hate work so much you go to a doctor who in his fucking wisdom decides you have a chemical imbalance in the fucking brain and prescribes you mind fucking pills. Did you have a chemical imbalance in the fucking brain before you were put in a mind-fucking cesspit?

No, I didn't fucking think so. So don't break your brain with chemicals. Get out of the fucking cesspit. You might find the imbalance in the brain suddenly comes good...

Being a Partner

You should not really have being a Partner as a goal. That's fucking hard, because you are probably one driven mother-fucker, and that is a box you want to tick, because…. well because of your ego really.

Whether or not it is a good thing will depend on all the circumstances: you, your firm, your appetite for risk and the rest of it. Make no mistake. The Partners, whose company you so fervently desire, are a pack of the evilest cunts imaginable. They are soulless monsters, whose closest relation in the modern world is the psychopath. They completely believe in their own right to rule, and that everyone else exists to serve.

I knew one cold fish who put her son in a boarding school in the same town in which she worked.

I knew another fat, alcoholic egomaniac in London who used to inject himself with a drug derived from the Komodo Dragon in order to suppress his hunger before having breakfast, lunch and dinner at a 3 Michelin star restaurants.

He looked 55 at 40 and fired or drove away every person who ever worked with him.

In his own mind: a highly successful lawyer, as evidenced by flash cars and a large real estate debt. In everyone else's mind: a complete loser; a vile specimen of a human being who incited disgust in anyone who met him.

Sure. You can join them. But they will take you for everything you've got. Your passions. Your humanity. Your pride. Your sense of self worth. Everything that was good about you at 20 will disappear, and you will either burn out, ruin your health or end up the very creature you swore not to be when you first started in the law.

There is another reason to become a Partner, if you must: the money. The trick is to operate like a navy seal – get in, get the cash, and get out. Whatever you do, don't fall into the lifestyle trap of buying more expensive crap to impress these fuckwits. It is a race you cannot win. Instead, to the extent possible, do not increase your lifestyle at all. Stash the fucking cash away. Don't drink it. Don't buy expensive cars or homes.

Stash the fucking cash away.

Read up on early retirement, if you end up on the big bucks. Google it. There is plenty out there. If you end up on good money, in less than 5 years you can stash away enough cash to get out and save your soul.

And still have time left to live your life.

The legal profession is full of old, sad bastards who have missed the boat. Their life – and all *life* entails – has sailed them by. Sure, they have a fistful of cash. Many fistfuls. But really, if you think of a wonderful life, or a wonderful time – what do you imagine?

Some 55 year old fat guy who has a superiority complex but can't relate to anyone?

No way! And if he's on a big yacht or in a convertible then he's even more tragic.

He is just one sad fuck.

No, the best things in life really can't be purchased with cash. In fact the main wonder of life doesn't have to be (and can't be) purchased at all: *time*. You're rich in time baby, and that's what those silly old cunts don't have.

Time to enjoy the sunshine. Time to enjoy beautiful food. Time to laugh with friends and hug your family. Time to take the girlfriend or boyfriend to the beach.

That's priceless! Don't undervalue it. You're already rich.

Money without time is meaningless.

Getting knifed

If you stay in the law long enough, you will be knifed. All around you, throughout your career, people will be being knifed.

You know that partner who decided to move on to another firm?

Knifed.

The senior lawyer who also decided to try another firm after a pretty quiet period?

Knifed.

Indeed, as you climb up the greasy pole you will be involved in your own knifings – seems unlikely and horrifying, but it will happen. Someone will be your competitor. Someone (many people) will try and *fuck you up*. Others in your group will be ruining the profitability you need to get the big fat pay rise, or to hang on to the dollars you have managed to extract from the system.

That's what it comes down to at the end of the day. Dollars.

Would you fuck up (knife) your friend for 20 bucks? Probably not.

What about 20 million.

For fucking sure.

What about 20 grand?

200?

As they say, everyone's a whore, name your price. If you survive in the system long enough, you will knife people. If you don't, it just means you are letting someone else do your dirty work for you, or you are looking to get knifed yourself.

It can hurt, getting knifed. Who likes getting knifed by your friends? Well, that's the thing. They were never your friends. It's like one big fucking episode of Game of Thrones: You Win or You Die. Trust nobody. Your friends will fuck you. Your lawyers will fuck you. Everyone, given the opportunity, will fuck you.

Why should you be king, after all?

It still hurts. How to handle it? Well, accept it's karma baby. You live by the sword…. and all the rest. And have a rich life outside of the law. That's where those old fuckers fall down. I remember one stupid old cunt thought he was the shit – real arrogant bastard – until he dropped dead in a car park at 55.

Not so fucking clever now hey old man. All that money doesn't count for shit now does it.

Anyway, back these old fuckers. They derive their entire sense worth from their wealth and vocation – in other words, nothing. They have no real friends (only fake friends). They often have a trophy wife. They have debt. They all have debt.

How can a cunt on a million bucks a year have debt?

I've fucking seen it. They think they are Gods, and spend accordingly. Earning money that should see them kept *forever* at a wonderful standard of living but they buy stupid shit that traps them!

Retired by 40 should be your goal if you stay in this insane game.

Get the fuck out.

Buy a fucking modest house. Keep your expenses low. Get out of the fucking nightmare, even if you are a fucking Partner.

Especially if you are a fucking Partner.

Get out, get out, get out.

One last thing, if they have a buy-in price – equity – then be very fucking careful and get out even earlier. Equity is just an invention to give the old cunts a payout on the way out. Be very careful. Very fucking careful. Those old cunts saw you, and your money, coming 20 years ago. They did not devise the system to protect your interests but theirs. There is every chance you will left holding a stinking, rotting turd once the last of those old cunts disappears waving their equity check.

The thing to do: fuck them, instead of the other way around. Yeah pay the buy-in price. Give them the fucking money. But do a dash and run, earn the cash and make them buy *your equity* a few years later, when you've stashed away enough to retire on and they are still drooling in their cereal every morning as they work to pay off their fucking debts and impress their dickhead neighbors.

It's a gamble, but often a law firm will last a few years or so and that's all you need.

Get the fuck in, take the cash, and get the fuck out.

By 40.

If you're still working in a law firm after 40 you've got rocks in your fucking head.

Or you're *one of them*.

Epilogue

I write this, in my forty fourth year, on a weekday. All of the silly fuckers I worked with for the better part of 20 years are at work, noses to the grindstone, playing their silly games and trying to work out which of them will die with the most toys.

They all hate each other. And themselves.

But I've left all that behind. I've got plenty to keep me busy. It really isn't that hard to make a living these days, so long as you leave your ego at the door and have a brain at your head.

I'm making plans. Cooking. Travelling. Family things.

Important things.

After all, I have the time.

Will you?

www.ingramcontent.com/pod-product-compliance
Lightning Source LLC
Chambersburg PA
CBHW070920210326
41521CB00010B/2252